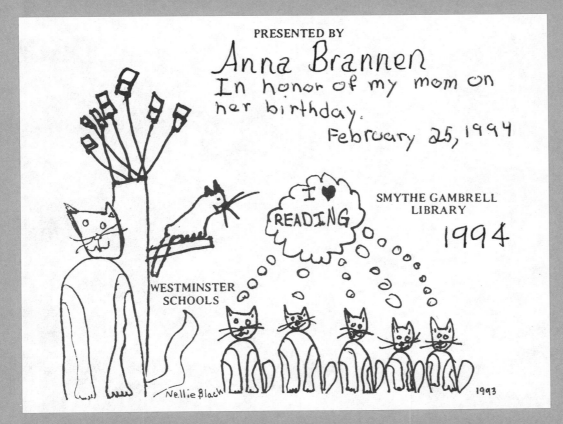

PRESENTED BY

Anna Brannen
In honor of my mom on her birthday.
February 25, 1994

I ♥ READING

SMYTHE GAMBRELL LIBRARY

1994

WESTMINSTER SCHOOLS

Nellie Black

1993

MAKE A SPLASH!

THOMPSON YARDLEY

MAKE A SPLASH!

THE MILLBROOK PRESS · BROOKFIELD, CONNECTICUT

Library of Congress Cataloging-in-Publication Data

Yardley, Thompson, 1951–
Make a splash! : care about the ocean / by Thompson Yardley.
p.   cm.—(A Lighter look book)
Includes bibliographical references and index.
Summary: Explores the ocean, industries and recreational
activities connected with it, and the threat posed by human
destruction of the environment.
ISBN 1-56294-147-X
1. Ocean—Juvenile literature.   [1. Ocean.]   I. Title.
II. Series.
GC21.5.Y37   1992
551.46—dc20   91-22963   CIP   AC

First published in the United States in 1992 by
The Millbrook Press
2 Old New Milford Road
Brookfield, Connecticut 06804
© Copyright Cassell plc 1991
First published in Great Britain in 1991 by
Cassell Publishers Limited

MAKE A SPLASH!

IN THE DRINK!

The sea isn't just a lot of blue, salty water. It's home for all sorts of living things.

And it's not always blue! Seawater is often green because there are billions of tiny green plants living in it.

But to know what really goes on in the water, you have to look beneath the surface. Take a dip in the sea and find out:

How to help wildlife!

How to find old coins!

Why the sea is salty!

What whales sing about!

TO THE BEACH

That's why it gets so crowded! You have to keep
your eyes open to spot strange and interesting creatures . . .

WELCOME TO QUIZ BEACH!

How many three-legged people
can you see in this picture?

You probably know how to make sandcastles with a bucket and a shovel.
But why not go for something more adventurous?

HOW TO MAKE SAND SCULPTURES

1. Find an uncrowded bit of beach. Make a big heap of damp sand.

2. Use your hands to mold it into the shape you want.

3. Try using seashells for eyes and seaweed for hair.

4. Add other items that you may find on the beach.

5. Stand back and watch people admire your work!

CLIFF HANGERS

Sandy beaches often form where rocks and cliffs are worn down by the sea. Sometimes the base of the cliff is eaten away—leaving a dangerous overhang that you can't see. This bit could break off at any time!

So keep away from the edge of cliffs!

Seabirds often make nests on cliffs and rocks. If you frighten them, they may leave their eggs unprotected.

Tell someone where you're headed before you go off!

Cliffs provide homes for all sorts of plants and animals. Cliff plants have strong roots to grip onto the rocks. But they may not be strong enough to support your weight!

If you go exploring, watch out for falling rocks! And keep an eye on the sea. The tide may come in and trap you. You may be lucky and be rescued. Or perhaps you won't!

SHELL SHELTERS

As the sea wears away cliffs, it washes out old rocks. Some of these are fossils—the stony remains of ancient animals. Some of them look like present-day shells. Shells are the self-made homes of living creatures called mollusks. Mollusks collect calcium for their shells from limestone rocks that have dissolved in the sea.

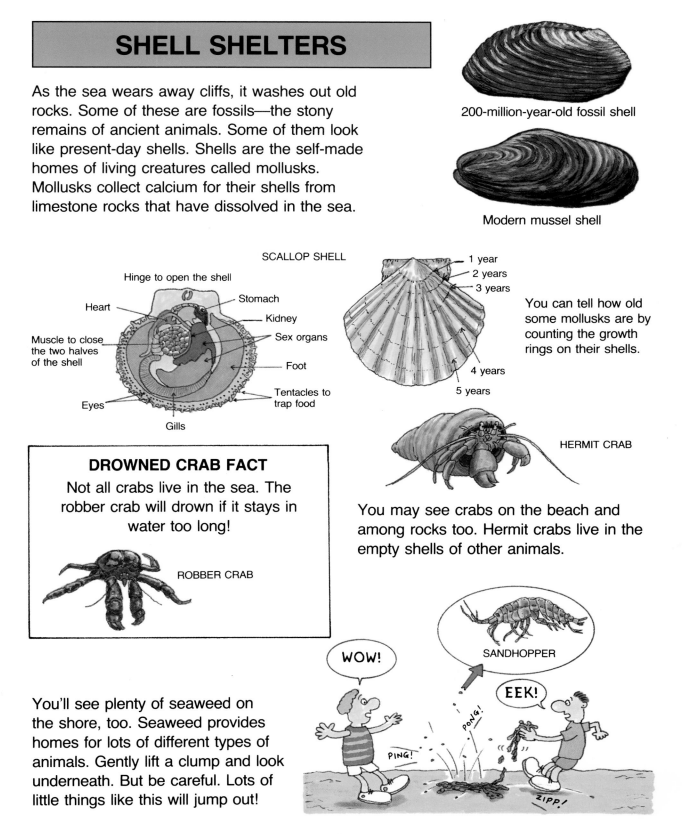

200-million-year-old fossil shell

Modern mussel shell

SCALLOP SHELL

Hinge to open the shell

Heart

Stomach

Kidney

Muscle to close the two halves of the shell

Sex organs

Foot

Eyes

Tentacles to trap food

Gills

1 year
2 years
3 years

4 years
5 years

You can tell how old some mollusks are by counting the growth rings on their shells.

HERMIT CRAB

You may see crabs on the beach and among rocks too. Hermit crabs live in the empty shells of other animals.

DROWNED CRAB FACT

Not all crabs live in the sea. The robber crab will drown if it stays in water too long!

ROBBER CRAB

WOW!

EEK!

SANDHOPPER

PING!

PONG!

ZIPP!

You'll see plenty of seaweed on the shore, too. Seaweed provides homes for lots of different types of animals. Gently lift a clump and look underneath. But be careful. Lots of little things like this will jump out!

BEACHCOMBING

Not just plants and animals are washed up on the beach. People have been dropping things in the sea for thousands of years . . .

Treasure from old wrecks

Old coins

Bottles with messages inside

Some people make a living searching for washed-up items on beaches. This is called beachcombing . . .

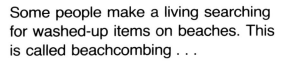

. . . but they don't do it like this!

HOW TO BEACHCOMB

1. Always watch where you're walking.

2. Look out for clumps of washed-up items. These are called flotsam.

3. Items of the same size and weight are often washed up in the same place. Look out for patches of small pebbles. You may be lucky and find modern coins or jewelry.

FINDING METAL

Modern treasure hunters use metal detectors to find all kinds of buried valuables—old iron tools, lost jewelry . . . even tiny flecks of gold at the bottom of streams!

A metal detector is an electronic device that looks like a long stick with a plastic disk at one end and a control box at the other. A coil inside the disk sends out a radio signal. When the signal strikes anything made of metal, it bounces back to a second coil in the disk, and a receiver inside the control box makes a loud beep.

The detector can find metal buried even a few inches down and tell you where to dig.

You might try searching for coins with a metal detector. But be careful how you use it.

1. Don't forget to fill in any holes you make.

2. Don't disturb other people who want to use the beach.

3. You'll find a lot of cans, pop-tops, and bottle caps. Don't just throw this trash back onto the beach!

Put it into a trash can. Or take it home for recycling!

DUNES AND DUMPERS

You'll find lots of litter on crowded beaches and in sand dunes. Picnic trash spoils everybody's fun. So . . . don't be a dune dumper!

Seagulls have very good eyesight!

BOTTLES
Take your bottles home with you.

GARBAGE
Leftover food and food containers attract flies and stinging insects. Wasp stings and sandfly bites are very painful. Put your leftover food in a trash can. Or feed the seagulls with it!

CANS
Sharp-edged metal cans are a menace too. Always take all of your cans home with you.

CAN-COLLECTING FACT

Some communities sponsor can-recycling programs. The person who collects the most gets an award from the local council. This helps to keep beaches free of cans.

ALL WASHED UP!

You may find other sorts of trash on beaches too . . .

CONTAINERS
Ships often carry freight containers on their decks. About three hundred of them are lost overboard every year. One may end up on your beach. Never try to open a container. There may be something dangerous inside!

LUMPS OF OIL
Sometimes you'll see lumps of crude oil like this. Oil often leaks from oil tankers and other ships. It can stick to birds' feathers and stop them from flying. Oil can also stick to you!

If you find an oily bird on your beach, call the local animal rescue society.

HOW TO CLEAN OFF OIL
You can use some types of suntan lotion to loosen oil on your skin. Mix it with some fine sand and rub it on gently. Then wash it off in the sea.

DUMPING TOWNS

Some towns on the coast use the ocean as a garbage dump. Millions of tons of household waste are dropped into the sea every year. About half of it is paper, cardboard, and waste food. This is called organic waste.

There are billions of tiny life-forms called plankton in the sea. Plankton can eat organic waste.

Dolphins, seals, and seabirds may get caught up in trash such as plastic bags.

But . . . plankton can't eat the other half of the trash. This includes plastic, rubber, metals, and household chemicals. So this trash is often washed back onto the beach.

SEWAGE
Human waste products are called sewage. Sometimes raw sewage is pumped straight into the sea. You can catch diseases from sewage. So . . . it's best not to play near sewage drains like this . . .

DUMPING SHIPS

Ships pollute the sea too. Oil tankers carry up to two hundred thousand tons of crude oil at a time! When they're not carrying oil, seawater is pumped into the empty tanks. This stops the ship from rolling about too much.

eek!

This seawater mixes with the leftover oil. Later, the tanks are emptied to make room for more oil. So the leftover oil is pumped into the sea too. Tankers pump about three quarters of a million tons of oil into the sea each year.

Many other poisonous wastes are dumped into the sea. Drums of chemicals may wash up on your beach. Some are marked with symbols that tell you that the contents are dangerous. But some drums don't have any warning sign at all!

SPOT THE DANGEROUS DRUM!

Which of these washed-up drums are safe to go near?

ANSWER:

Only drum F, because: A = The contents will burn you. B = Deadly poison. C = More deadly poison! D = Radioactive waste. E = You don't know what's inside!

THE FOOD CHAIN

All the living things in the sea depend on each other for food. Big fish eat small fish. Small fish eat tiny fish, and so on. This is called a food chain. Here's an example:

2. Smaller fish such as sardines live by eating animal plankton. Sardines live for about twelve years. One sardine may eat millions of tiny animals in that time.

1. The largest tuna grow to about 9½ feet (3 meters) long. They weigh up to 1,220 pounds (550 kilograms) and live up to fifteen years. One tuna may eat a hundred thousand small fish such as sardines in that time.

Two types of plant plankton magnified fifty times

Dinoflagellates

Diatoms

Diatoms

3. There are many different types of animal plankton. They live by eating plant plankton. One tiny animal may eat thousands of plants in its lifetime.

Two types of animal plankton magnified fifteen times

Copepod

Pteropod

4. There are billions of tiny plants in the sea. The droppings from fish provide food for the tiny plants.

People come into this food chain too. You may have eaten tuna or sardines recently. But . . . we have to be careful not to break the food chain. What happens if we catch too many sardines, for example? The tuna will have less to eat and may starve to death. And . . . more animal plankton will survive and eat more plants. Then there'll be fewer plants!

Humph!... No sardines to eat! I'm starving!

Tuna

Animal plankton

Goody goody! No sardines to eat us!

And we have to be careful not to poison the food chain, too!

Almost all the Earth's water is in the sea. People who dump chemical wastes in it say that a few extra tons of poisons won't make any difference.

But they're wrong!

Deadly poisons such as lead and mercury may collect inside plants and animals in the sea. When the larger animals eat them they take in the poison too!

FOOD CHAIN POISON PUZZLE!

Take another look at the food chain on the opposite page. Imagine:

1. If each plant plankton eats a particle of poison from a leaking drum of waste . . .

2. If each animal plankton eats a thousand plant plankton . . .

3. If each sardine eats a million tiny animals . . .

4. If each tuna eats a hundred thousand sardines . . .

How many particles of chemical waste will there be inside the tuna?

ANSWER: 100,000,000,000,000,000,000

MINAMATA MERCURY FACT

In the 1950s a factory in Japan dumped mercury waste in the sea. It got into the local food chain and poisoned people in a fishing port called Minamata. Mercury damages the brain and the nerves.

BUT . . . accidents like this don't happen very often. So don't worry too much—fresh fish are still safe to eat!

FISH FACTS

Fishing boats catch about eighty million tons of fish each year. There are about thirty thousand different sorts of fish. But in the United States we use only about one hundred different types for food.

This fishing ship is called a stern trawler.

School of sardines

Some fish, such as tuna, are big enough to catch with a fishing rod. But most of the fish we eat are caught with nets.

Some types of fish swim in groups called schools. So a big net can catch thousands of fish at once. Some types of fish are in danger of dying out because we catch too many of them.

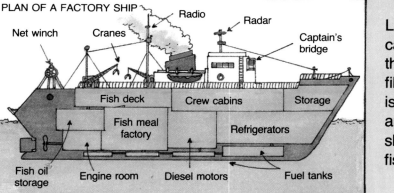

PLAN OF A FACTORY SHIP

Net winch   Cranes   Radio   Radar   Captain's bridge

Fish deck   Crew cabins   Storage
Fish meal factory   Refrigerators
Fish oil storage   Engine room   Diesel motors   Fuel tanks

Large modern fishing boats are called factory ships. They turn the fish into fish meal, fish fillets, and fish sticks. Fish meal is made into food for farm animals. Overfishing by factory ships can badly affect local fishing industries.

DANGEROUS DRIFT-NET FACT
Some fishing ships use large drift nets. They catch any fish that happen along. But . . . they often trap whales, dolphins, and seals too! These animals can easily drown in a drift net because they need to breathe air.

OCEAN EXPERT FISHING CODE

1. Catch fish only to eat, not for fun.

2. Put young, small fish back in the water so that they get a chance to grow.

3. Try eating different types of fish for a change.

WHALES AND SHARKS

WHALES

Whales, dolphins, and seals aren't fish. They're mammals. A mammal is an animal that produces milk for its young. The blue whale can weigh up to 160 tons and is the largest animal—ever—in the world. A baby blue whale needs about half a ton of milk a day! Until recently, whaling ships caught so many whales that some types almost died out. Nowadays, most whales are protected by international law.

SHARKS

There are three hundred and eighty different types of sharks. Some types will eat you if they catch you! Here are three dangerous ones:

HUMPBACK WHALE FACT

Some whales are able to find food by making loud noises. They listen to the echoes that bounce back to them. They can recognize objects this way. Humpback whales also sing to each other over long distances to find a mate.

Great white shark grows up to 40 feet (12 meters) long.

Tiger shark grows up to 20 feet (6 meters) long.

Blue shark grows up to 15 feet (4.5 meters) long.

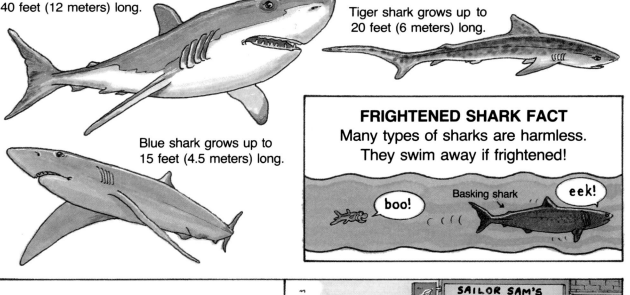

FRIGHTENED SHARK FACT

Many types of sharks are harmless. They swim away if frightened!

boo!

Basking shark

eek!

SHARK STEAK FACT

More sharks are eaten by people than people are eaten by sharks!

SAILOR SAM'S FISH BISTRO

SPECIAL TODAY SHARK AND FRIES!

SEAFOOD

Besides fish, we can eat all sorts of other seafood:

SEAWEED
Seaweed contains valuable food chemicals such as iodine. Some types are grown on seaweed farms in Japan.

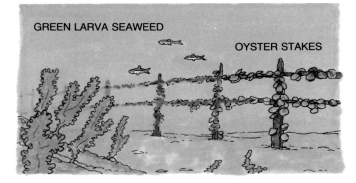

Sometimes valuable pearls form inside oysters!

SHELLFISH
Shellfish such as oysters and mussels are also grown for food. Oyster farmers put wooden stakes into the seabed. The oysters attach themselves to the stakes. The shellfish are collected when they're big enough to eat.

LOBSTERS
We also eat larger animals such as crabs and lobsters. Lobster catchers use lobster pots to trap them. They work like this:

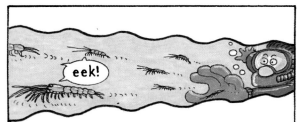

KRILL CATCH FEAR FACT

Krill are distant relatives of lobsters. They look like tiny shrimp, and are food for some whales and fish. Fishing vessels catch about 500,000 tons of krill each year. Some sea experts are worried that we are catching too many krill. The more krill people eat, the less there are for the other sea animals to live on.

1. The lobster sees or smells the dead fish bait in the lobster pot.

2. It climbs in the trapdoor on the top to eat the bait.

3. The door springs shut and the lobster can't get out.

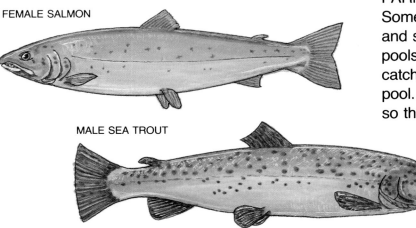

FEMALE SALMON

MALE SEA TROUT

FARM FISH

Some types of fish such as trout and salmon are grown in large pools on fish farms. It's easier to catch them if they're in an artificial pool. They're fed with special food so that they grow quickly.

What flavor are you?

STRAWBERRY!

Oh! I thought you were a Lemon Sole!

The type of food they eat also affects what they taste like. Some fish farmers try to improve the taste of fish by adding chemical flavors to fish food!

BE AN EXPERT FISH EATER!

Fresh seafood is usually very good for your health. But some fish are poisonous. And some parts of a fish are poisonous too. If you catch your own fish to eat:

1. Don't eat anything unless you know what it is.

2. Make sure all the insides are cut out before you cook it.

3. Watch out for bones!

1. WOW! It must be a Boot Fish! Ahah!

2. SCHLOOOP! YUK!

3. KOFF! OOOO!

FUN AT SEA

Large ships and boats are used for fishing and transportation. These days, most small boats are used for pleasure . . .

Fishing

GOT ONE!

Silly humans!

Quiet sunbathing

Water-skiing

WAP!

Racing

But motorboats are bad for wildlife. The outboard motors can injure and kill slow-moving animals and fish. Manatees are mammals that eat plants in shallow water. They are often found with propeller scars on their backs.

SAILING
Sailboats are more healthful and can be more fun than motorboats. They are powered by the wind instead of by smoky motors.

TOOT! TOOT!

WINDSURFING

Windsurfing is great fun too. But you need to be an expert to do it properly.

Watch people windsurfing. You'll notice that they spend a lot of time falling in the water!

SURF FUN TIPS

Surfing is a lot harder than it looks!

At first find a beach with small waves and no rocks. A big wave can hit you with the force of a truckload of bricks!

If you lose your board, relax and let the waves carry you to the beach. Don't try to swim against the rip current. This is the wave water running back into the sea. Get to the beach by swimming alongside it. Take deep breaths when you can, and let the waves get you to the shore. Have fun!

Of course, for all these activities you need to be able to swim!

IN THE SWIM

Swimming is the best exercise for staying fit and healthy. You can get swimming lessons at many community centers and schools.

Swimming pools are easier to swim in than the sea. Practice diving and underwater swimming until you're good at it.

Once you've learned how to swim properly, take a dip in the sea. It's great fun sharing the water with other animals! Swimming in the sea is quite safe if you watch what you're doing.

Don't dive in without looking. You never know what's just beneath the surface!

IN THE DEEP

Fish breathe tiny bubbles of oxygen in water. They can't breathe air because it's not damp enough. And water's too damp for people to breathe! But you can use a snorkel to swim just under the surface. This helps you to breathe with your head beneath the water.

HOW TO TUBE-WATCH

If you can't swim, you can still watch the sea wildlife. It's hard to see through the surface ripples. So try this:

1. Get an old plastic bucket.
2. Cut out the bottom.
3. Use it like this . . .

ooo!

Some people join a scuba-diving club and learn how to swim underwater.

SNIFF!

Divers breathe from the tanks of compressed air that they carry on their backs. Seawater can be very cold a few yards down, so divers wear a rubber wet suit to help keep them warm. It also protects them from sharp rocks. A bleeding wound may attract dangerous fish such as sharks.

Fish float because they have a sac of air in their bodies.

DO YOU FLOAT?

Your body is just light enough to float in water too. That's partly because you contain trapped air. Air is lighter than water, so it helps you to float. You can see this working in the bath:

DREADFUL DROWNING FACT

WOW!

glub!

About a fifth of all accidental drownings happen in the home!

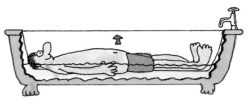

↑ Water level ↑
6 in

1. Keep your head above the water! Relax your body and breathe out. You'll sink a bit.

2. Keep your head above the water! Then breathe in, so your lungs are full of air. You'll find that your body floats higher in the water.

You can float better in the sea. The sea has lots of salt in it, so it's heavier than tap water.

| 1. Float a heavy piece of wood in a bowl of tap water. | 2. Pour in some table salt and stir it around. | 3. Now the wood floats higher in the water! |

WHY THE SEA IS SALTY FACT

Seawater and rocks contain thousands of different chemicals. These are washed from the land to the sea by rivers. The most common of these chemicals is called sodium chloride. This is better known as table salt!

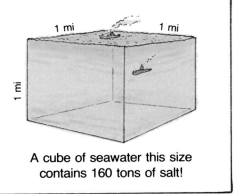

1 mi   1 mi

1 mi

A cube of seawater this size contains 160 tons of salt!

A PINCH OF SALT

Most fish that live in the sea can't live in fresh water. They need the salt that passes through their bodies. Sodium in salt helps their nerves to carry messages. All animals have nerves, and they all need salt to stay alive.

SALTWATER-FISH FLESH FACT

Saltwater fish don't contain much salt. Their bodies don't need to store it because they live in salty water.

A quart of blood contains about the same amount of salt as a quart of seawater.

But freshwater fish and land animals don't live in salty water. So they have to carry their own supply of salt with them. Next time you cut yourself, taste your blood. It's a bit salty!

In some parts of the world, people collect salt from the sea . . .

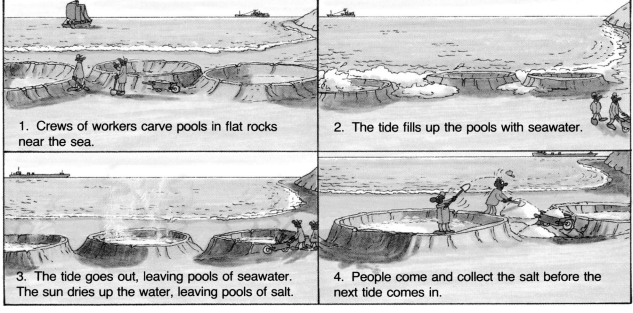

1. Crews of workers carve pools in flat rocks near the sea.

2. The tide fills up the pools with seawater.

3. The tide goes out, leaving pools of seawater. The sun dries up the water, leaving pools of salt.

4. People come and collect the salt before the next tide comes in.

TIME AND TIDE

All objects in the universe attract each other with a force called gravity. You are being attracted by the Earth when you fall out of a tree!

The Earth attracts the moon and the moon attracts the Earth. But don't worry—the moon won't fall on the Earth!

The moon travels around the Earth once every twenty-eight days. It's traveling just fast enough to stop it from falling on the Earth. And it's traveling just slow enough to stop it from flying off into space!

Moon

Earth

What's he saying?

The sea bulges out here (high tide).

(NOT TO SCALE)

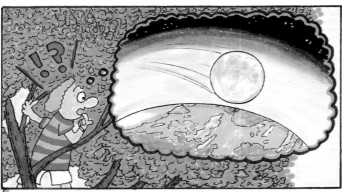

Earth

Moon's gravity

Moon

The sea becomes shallower here (low tide).

About three quarters of the Earth's surface is water. The moon's gravity is strong enough to slightly attract this water and make it bulge. The Earth spins once every twenty-four hours. The bulge is always directly underneath the moon. This is what causes high and low tides. But that's not all . . .

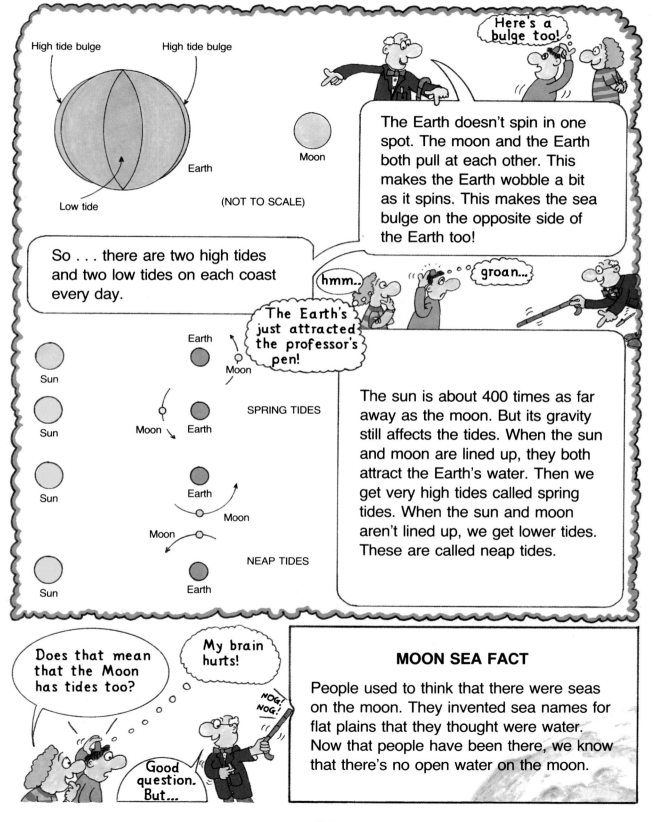

ICE AND WATER

The sun does more than help to make tides. It also heats up the sea, making the water move in currents. These currents can move floating objects for thousands of miles.

Some parts of the world don't get much sunshine. So at the North and South poles for example, water freezes. A thick layer of ice and snow called an ice cap forms. Large chunks break off and float away on the currents. These chunks are called icebergs.

There are billions of gallons of frozen water in the ice caps. If it all melted, the sea level would rise. Some scientists think that coastlines would be flooded with 150 feet (50 meters) of water. And many of the world's big cities are near the coast!

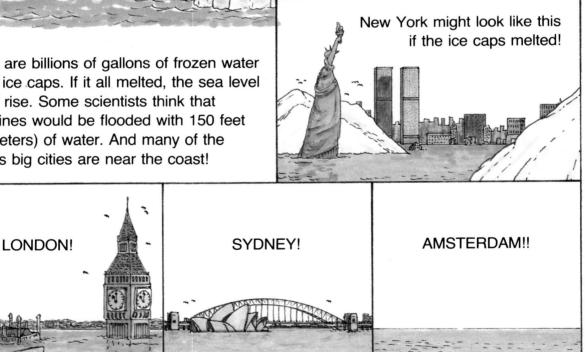

New York might look like this if the ice caps melted!

LONDON!

SYDNEY!

AMSTERDAM!!

This could happen because weather experts say that the Earth is getting warmer!

THIS IS BECAUSE OF THE GREENHOUSE EFFECT!

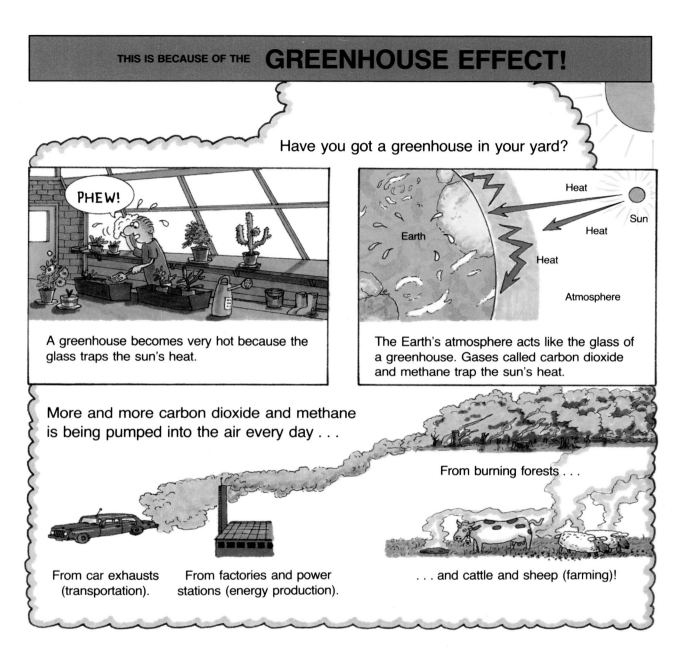

Have you got a greenhouse in your yard?

A greenhouse becomes very hot because the glass traps the sun's heat.

Heat
Sun
Heat
Earth
Heat
Atmosphere

The Earth's atmosphere acts like the glass of a greenhouse. Gases called carbon dioxide and methane trap the sun's heat.

More and more carbon dioxide and methane is being pumped into the air every day . . .

From burning forests . . .

From car exhausts (transportation).

From factories and power stations (energy production).

. . . and cattle and sheep (farming)!

So more and more heat is trapped in the atmosphere!

HELPING THE ICE CAPS

SNIFF! SNIFF! ← oxygen

You can help to slow the greenhouse effect:

1. Get your parents and friends to use their cars less.

2. Use less energy. Remember to turn off lights and TVs.

3. Plants take in carbon dioxide and produce oxygen. So . . . plant some trees!

THE WATER CYCLE

The sun makes the world's water go round and round. This is called the water cycle. It works like this:

1. The sun heats up the sea. Steam rises to form clouds.

2. The wind blows the clouds toward the land.

3. The clouds reach cool air. Sometimes this is over the sea, sometimes over the land. The clouds become heavy with water. Rain falls. Rivers take the rainwater back to the sea.

Nice cup of tea

Steam

Ice

Metal tray

Boil some water near a bowl of ice.

The steam cools and turns to water on the cold bowl. Water collects in the tray.

You can see a water cycle happening in your own home. Get an adult to help you with this experiment.

You can empty the tray of water back into the kettle. Then start again!

Streams and rivers join together to form a large river near the coast. This wide tidal part is called an estuary. All sorts of plants and wildlife live in estuaries.

Rain

Rivers

Estuary

ESTUARIES

But . . . people like to use estuaries, too! They build boat marinas, campsites, hotels, resorts, and so on. The pollution from these activities can ruin estuaries. Poisonous chemicals that farmers use can drain into estuaries. And rivers bring pollution from towns upstream, too!

BE AN ESTUARY SAVER!

1. Never throw trash into estuaries or rivers.

2. Don't disturb wildlife, especially birds and their eggs. Lots of people used to collect birds' eggs. Some types of birds have died out because of egg collecting. Some eggs are protected by law!

BE A WILDLIFE SAVER!
Some of the world's estuaries have been made into nature reserves to protect wildlife. Other places need looking after, too. And you can help. Start a wildlife protection club at your school. Then you can help look after local wildlife when you come back from the beach!

Wildlife protection club in action!

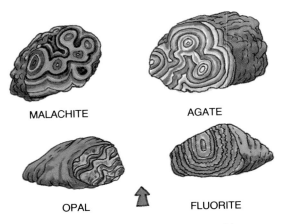

MALACHITE

AGATE

OPAL

FLUORITE

These stones have been cut with a special saw, then polished.

Why not start a rock collection? You'll find lots of beautiful pebbles on most beaches. Some very ordinary-looking stones have amazing patterns inside. Break a few open with a sharp hammer and see.

Collect some empty shells too. Then you can make models of animals and other things with them!

GLUE

teacher

EEK!

SEA-URCHINS CHEAP!

CONCHES ~ SPECIAL OFFER!

You can buy stones from beach souvenir shops, but it's not a good idea to buy shells. Conch and sea-urchin shells look very pretty, but they aren't often washed up on the beach in one piece. So people dive and collect these shells from the seabed. Then the animals inside are boiled alive to kill them, leaving the shells. This is not good for the food chain.

THE BARRIER REEF STORY

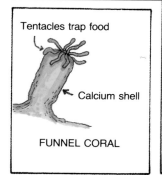

Tentacles trap food

Calcium shell

FUNNEL CORAL

Tiny animals called corals also have shells. They are made of calcium too. Each type clumps together in different ways to form odd growths. They look a bit like stone plants!

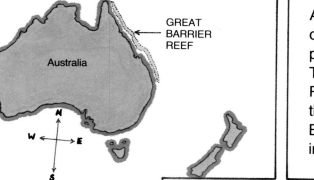

GREAT BARRIER REEF

Australia

N
W — E
S

As old corals die, new ones grow on top of them. After thousands of years, huge piles of corals called coral reefs form. The largest one is the Great Barrier Reef, near Australia. This is a home for thousands of types of sea life.
But look what happens when tourists interfere with the reef . . .

Spiky starfish called the crown of thorns eat corals.

MUNCH! MUNCH!

Shellfish called tritons eat these starfish.

eek!

LEAP!

But . . . divers collect tritons to sell to tourists.

So with fewer tritons around, the starfish can eat more corals.

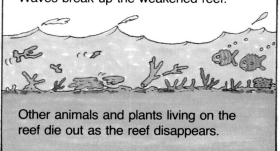

The corals can't grow quickly enough. Waves break up the weakened reef.

Other animals and plants living on the reef die out as the reef disappears.

So . . . tourists taking just a few souvenirs home can damage other wildlife too! You can pick up souvenirs from the beach . . .

But make sure they're dead first!

NIP!!

nnn!

FIND OUT MORE

Now that you've learned how important the sea is, you may want to find out more about the things that live in it. Here are some books to look for in the library:

The Bottom of the Sea, by Augusta Goldin (Crowell, 1967)

Dive to the Coral Reefs, by Elizabeth Tayntor, Paul Erickson and Les Kaufman (Crown, 1986)

Ocean World, by Tony Rice (Millbrook, 1991)

The Seashore, by Joyce Pope (Franklin Watts, 1985)

INDEX